EVOLUTION OF COASTAL STRUCTURES

JAMAICA BAY PAMPHLET LIBRARY 14

EVOLUTION OF COASTAL STRUCTURES

STRUCTURES OF COASTAL RESILIENCE

Jamaica Bay Team
Spitzer School of Architecture
The City College of New York

Catherine Seavitt Nordenson, editor
Associate Professor of Landscape Architecture

Kjirsten Alexander
Research Associate

Danae Alessi
Research Associate

Eli Sands
Research Assistant

JAMAICA BAY PAMPHLET LIBRARY
14 Evolution of Coastal Structures

ISBN 978-1-942900-14-6

CONTACT
Catherine Seavitt Nordenson
cseavittnordenson@ccny.cuny.edu
www.structuresofcoastalresilience.org

SCR Jamaica Bay Team
The City College of New York
Spitzer School of Architecture
Program in Landscape Architecture, Room 2M24A
141 Convent Avenue New York, New York 10031

COVER
Breakwater. W.S. Bates, 1886. US Patent No 346140.
source: U.S. Patent Archive

supported by

89th Congress, 1st Session – – – – – – – – – – House Document No. 215

ATLANTIC COAST OF NEW YORK CITY FROM EAST ROCKAWAY INLET TO ROCKAWAY INLET AND JAMAICA BAY, NEW YORK

LETTER

FROM

THE SECRETARY OF THE ARMY

TRANSMITTING

A LETTER FROM THE CHIEF OF ENGINEERS, DEPART-
MENT OF THE ARMY, DATED APRIL 26, 1965, SUBMITTING
A REPORT, TOGETHER WITH ACCOMPANYING PAPERS
AND ILLUSTRATIONS, ON A COOPERATIVE BEACH ERO-
SION CONTROL STUDY AND AN INTERIM HURRICANE
SURVEY OF THE ATLANTIC COAST OF NEW YORK CITY
FROM EAST ROCKAWAY INLET TO ROCKAWAY INLET
AND JAMAICA BAY, NEW YORK, AUTHORIZED BY THE
RIVER AND HARBOR ACT APPROVED JULY 3, 1930, AS
AMENDED AND SUPPLEMENTED, AND PUBLIC LAW 71,
84TH CONGRESS, APPROVED JUNE 15, 1955

JUNE 23, 1965.—Referred to the Committee on Public Works and
ordered to be printed with illustrations

U.S. GOVERNMENT PRINTING OFFICE
WASHINGTON : 1965

Transmittal letter from the Secretary of the Army, 1965
source: US Army Corps of Engineers, New York District

In 1965, the United States Army Corps of Engineers transmitted to Congress a beach erosion and hurricane study including three proposed plans of "improvement" for the Rockaway Peninsula and Jamaica Bay. The study, completed in the aftermath of extensive damage caused by Hurricane Donna in 1960 and a nor'easter in March 1962, identified serious losses from hurricanes and erosion and recommended engineered structural improvements for combined hurricane protection and beach erosion control. The study area consisted of the Atlantic Coast of New York City from East Rockaway Inlet to Rockaway Inlet and Jamaica Bay.

The US Army Corps has developed Coastal Protection Manuals since the 1950s, design reference manuals including calculations and typical sections for structural methods to provide protection against damage from the impacts of natural phenomena upon the coast. These typical sections were intended to be applied to various locations along the rapidly developing United States coastline; the application of these specifically calibrated sections were manifest as linear extrusions along massive lengths of undifferentiated shorelines. The Coastal Protection Manuals, updated periodically, were eventually morphed into USACE's Coastal Engineering Manual (CEM), still in use today.

Fifty years later, in the wake of extensive damages along the eastern seaboard caused by Hurricane Sandy, the US Army Corps is preparing its submission of the North Atlantic Coast Comprehensive Study to Congress in January 2015. It is striking to note the paradigm shift from the use of the typical engineered section in the 1965 study to the growing interest in the use of natural and nature-based features (NNBF) as part of coastal storm risk reduction. New concepts have also emerged from the Corps' Engineer Research and Development Center (ERDC), emphasizing "Engineering with Nature" rather than against it.

The notion of a USACE structural "improvement" is a creative and inventive act of design, one honed through time and successive manuals developed by USACE engineers. Yet improvements have trended toward an acceptance of a particular formulaic approach to coastal protection inherent in the design manual.

But the inventor's mind is a flexible one. Delving into the nineteenth-century United States Patent and Trademark Office archives reveals reams of ordinary citizens' patent applications for coastal and riverine inventions and improvements. These structures often include strategies that work with the natural forces of waves, current, and sedimentation. The intentions of these inventors, seen in their descriptions of the various apparatuses, are less about control than the harnessing and manipulation of natural processes and forces, revealing the creativity of the inventor's mind in the realm of the littoral edge. Many of the examples below were accessed through landscape architect Richard Hindle's extensive online catalog of historic landscape-related patents at http://dialecticalmaterial.com.

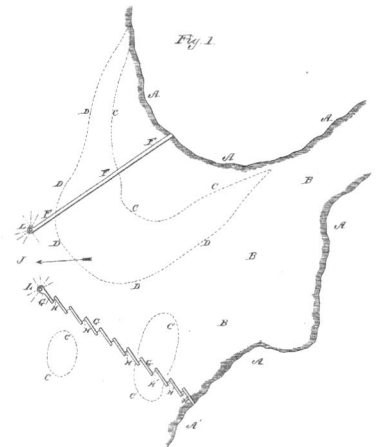

UNITED STATES PATENT OFFICE.

JOHN C. GOODRIDGE, JR., OF NEW YORK, N. Y.

PROCESS OF DEEPENING AND MAINTAINING CHANNELS FOR NAVIGATION.

SPECIFICATION forming part of Letters Patent No. 320,129, dated June 16, 1885.

Application filed March 5, 1885. (No model.)

To all whom it may concern:

Be it known that I, JOHN C. GOODRIDGE, Jr., of New York, in the county of New York and State of New York, have invented a new and useful Improvement in Process for the Deepening and Maintenance of Channels for Navigation, of which the following is a specification, reference being had to the accompanying drawings.

My invention relates to the employment of the scour of a natural current to deepen and maintain a channel for navigation. When the bed of a river or the bar of a harbor is of sand or other light material, beneficial result has heretofore followed the use of jetties so arranged as to localize the current and increase the rapidity of its flow, thus scouring out the sand and preventing the deposit of matter suspended in the water and borne down from above. But as far as harbors are concerned this improvement has in all cases been limited to those into which large rivers flow, and in which therefore the discharge on the ebb greatly exceeds the influx on the flood; but this is not the case with tidal harbors, for there the influx and efflux are substantially equal. To surmount this difficulty in these cases is the purpose of my invention. All action toward maintaining a channel must be toward the sea—that is, outward. This I propose to accomplish by making many points of inlet, thus obtaining a diffuse and gentle influx, then by impounding and embaying a large quantity of water, and so directing it on its outward passage that the greater portion of its volume is directed through the space desired as a channel, the conditions existing in those harbors fed by large rivers are practically reproduced, with a like beneficial effect.

Excerpt from patent application by John C. Goodridge, JR., 1885
source: US Patent and Trademark Office

CORPS OF ENGINEERS U.S. ARMY

LOCATION MAP
JAMAICA BAY, N.Y.
AND VICINITY
SCALE IN MILES

PROPOSED DIKE
TOP WIDTH 10 FT AT 15 FT M.S.L.
SIDE SLOPES 1 ON 2.5

PROPOSED LEVEE
TOP WIDTH 10 FT AT 15 FT M.S.L.
RIPRAPPED WATER SLOPE 1 ON 3
LAND SLOPE 1 ON 2.5

BARREN ISLAND
U.S. NAVAL AIR STATION

PROPOSED CONCRETE FLOOD WALL
TOP EL 15 FT M.S.L.

PROPOSED DIKE
TOP WIDTH 10 FT AT 15 FT M.S.L.
SIDE SLOPE 1 ON 2.5

PROPOSED STONE BARRIER
TOP WIDTH 12 FT AT EL 18 FT M.S.L.
TWO GATES 150 FT EACH

NAVIGATION INLET
300 FT WIDE WITH GATES CLOSED
500 FT WIDE WITH GATES OPEN

PROPOSED LEVEE
TOP WIDTH 10 FT AT EL 18 FT M.S.L. TO 15 FT M.S.L.
RIPRAPPED BOTH SIDES 1 ON 3

CLOSURE STRUCTURE
TWO SECTIONS, EACH 6 FT HIGH
AND 40 FT WIDE

PROPOSED CONCRETE FLOOD WALL
TOP EL 18.0 FT M.S.L.

PROPOSED BEACH FILL
BERM AT +10 FT M.S.L.
SHORE SLOPE 1 ON 20

NOTES
FOR DETAILS OF PLAN OF IMPROVEMENT SEE FIGURES K-1 TO K-17 OF APPENDIX K.
THE TOP ELEVATION OF THE PROPOSED HURRICANE BARRIER AND OCEAN FLOODWALL IS 18 FEET, MEAN SEA LEVEL,
AND THE TOP ELEVATION OF THE REMAINING IMPROVEMENT WORKS IS 15 FEET, MEAN SEA LEVEL.

LEGEND
HURRICANE BARRIER
LEVEES OR DIKES
FLOOD WALLS
CLOSURE STRUCTURES
ALIGNMENT REFERENCE LINE
BEACH FILL

COOPERATIVE BEACH EROSION CONTROL AND HURRICANE STUDY
EAST ROCKAWAY INLET TO ROCKAWAY INLET
AND JAMAICA BAY, NEW YORK
PLAN 1

SCALE IN FEET

PLATE 14

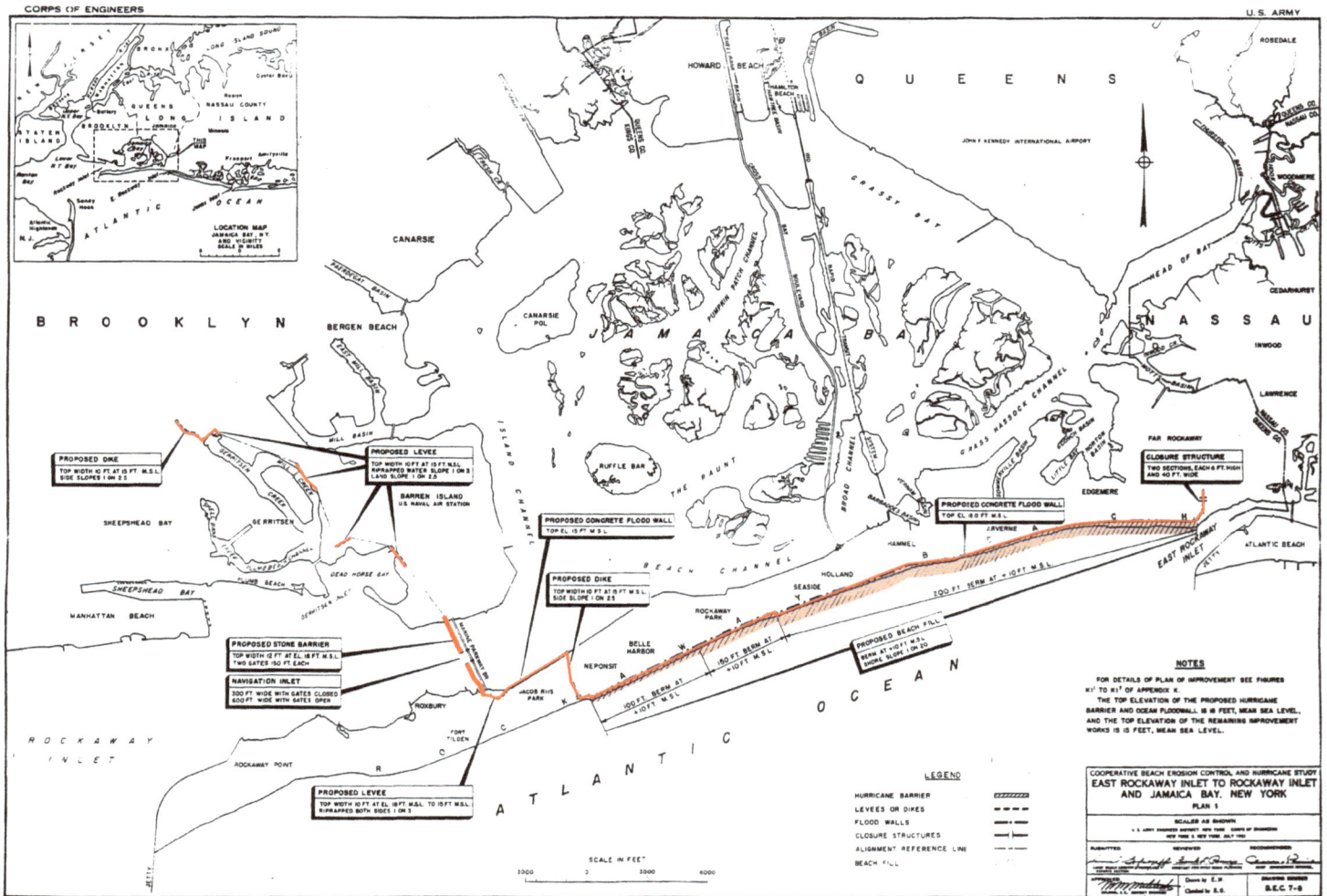

Cooperative Beach Erosion Control and Hurricane Study, 1965
East Rockaway Inlet to Rockaway Inlet and Jamaica Bay, PLAN 1
source: US Army Corps of Engineers, New York District

123. **Plan 1.** This plan, shown on plate 14 of the main report and figures K1¹ to K1⁷ of appendix K, provides generally for a hurricane barrier across the entrance to Jamaica Bay, a concrete wall and levee along Jamaica Bay adjacent to Jacob Riis Park, a dike and a concrete wall across the Rockaway peninsula from the north shore to the south shore, and a concrete wall fronted by a beach along the ocean front from the east end of Jacob Riis Park to the vicinity of Beach 19th Street near the east end of the Rockaway peninsula. A levee and dike system would tie the north end of the barrier into high ground in Brooklyn. A concrete wall would tie in the east end of the improvement to high ground at Beach 19th Street. Construction of groins for additional protection of beaches and reduction of fill losses has been considered. However, since the cost of the groins would be substantial and the expected saving in beach nourishment cannot be forecast with certainty (see paragraphs L13 and L13a, appendix L), no groins are included in the considered plans.

124. The proposed Jamaica Bay barrier would be a rock and sand fill structure 4,530 feet in length. It would extend across Rockaway Inlet from Jacob Riis Park in Rockaway to Marine Park in Brooklyn. The barrier would have a top elevation of 18 feet, mean sea level, a top width of 12 feet, and side slopes of 1 on 1.5. A gated opening 600 feet wide would be provided to accommodate navigation and allow for tidal circulation in the bay. The barrier would be provided with fishing platforms on both the ocean and bay sides, totaling about 6,000 feet in length. The elevation of the platforms would be 8 feet, mean sea level. Parking areas for fishermen would be provided at both ends of the barrier.

125. Partial closure of the navigation opening in the barrier to 300 feet would be accomplished by two rolling dam type gates with concrete abutments and sills. Each gate would have a height of 60.5 feet. The gate sills would be at an elevation of 42.5 feet below mean sea level (40 feet below mean low water). This sill elevation would permit future deepening of the navigation channel without requiring any modification of the structure. The maximum current in the navigation opening during the rise and fall of a spring tide has been determined to be about 4.5 knots. This maximum current, which would only occur during a few tidal cycles of each month, and then for only a short period of time, is not considered to be excessive from the standpoint of navigation.

126. Protection along the ocean front of the Rockaway peninsula would be provided by 32,100 feet of steel sheet piling encased in concrete with a top elevation of 18 feet, mean sea level, extending from the east end of Jacob Riis Park to the end of the timber boardwalk near Beach 19th Street. The wall would be fronted by a beach with a berm varying in width from 100 to 200 feet, depending on recreational needs, at an elevation of 10 feet, mean sea level, and foreshore slopes of 1 on 20 and 1 on 30. At Jacob Riis Park, the protection would be carried north to Jamaica Bay with 1,150 feet of I-wall and 2,100 feet of dike. Beach Channel Drive and Rockaway Beach Boulevard would be raised and a stoplog structure would be provided at the Neponsit Home for the Aged. At Beach 19th Street, the improvement would continue with an I-wall to high ground north of Seagirt Boulevard, a distance of 1,300 feet. A ramp would be provided at the boardwalk and a stoplog structure at Seagirt Boulevard. The top elevations of the structures at the west and east ends of the improvement would vary from 18 feet mean sea level at the ocean side to 15 feet at the inshore side. Levees would have a top width of 10 feet and side slopes of 1 on 3 and 1 on 2.5 on the exposed and protected sides, respectively. Dikes would have a top width of 10 feet and side slopes of 1 on 2.5.

127. Along Jamaica Bay, the improvement would be carried to high ground at the roadway interchange of the Marine Parkway Bridge by a concrete floodwall for a length of 3,400 feet and a levee for 1,100 feet. These structures would have top elevations of 15 feet above mean sea level. The levee would have a top width of 10 feet and side slopes of 1 on 3 with riprap protection on both sides.

128. The improvement north of the barrier structure would be carried to high ground in the Borough of Brooklyn near the intersection of Avenue S and Stuart Street by about 4,800 feet of levee and 1,700 feet of dike. These structures are either located on relatively high ground or at locations where they would not be exposed to wave heights as great as those affecting the proposed barrier across Rockaway Inlet. The levee would have a top width of 10 feet and a riprap slope of 1 on 3 on the exposed side. The protected side would have a slope of 1 on 2.5. The dike would have a top width of 10 feet with 1 on 2.5 side slopes.

129. The proposed structures have been designed to meet the conditions imposed by the occurrence of a standard project hurricane surge of 12.3 feet occurring at mean tide conditions. At the time of such a hurricane, with the barrier gates closed, thus constricting the navigation opening to 300 feet, this tide would be attenuated to 5.2 feet inside Jamaica Bay. This is just about the stage of zero damage in the bay. Some slight additional damage would be caused by the effect of wind set-up in the bay. However, this damage would occur very infrequently and would not be of sufficient magnitude to justify construction of local protective works in the bay. Damage from ocean inundation in Rockaway between Beach 19th Street and the east end of Jacob Riis Park would be eliminated for a design storm.

130. The maximum current of 4.5 knots that would be experienced in the navigation opening of the main barrier during a spring tide would not be objectionable to present or prospective commerce in Jamaica Bay. The proposed 600-foot wide opening and 40-foot mean low water depth are considered adequate for prospective commerce.

131. The United States Public Health Service has considered the effect of the barrier on pollution in Jamaica Bay. It has been concluded that the proposed barrier would result in little or no deterioration of water quality in Jamaica Bay which should not be detrimental to present and anticipated water uses (see paragraph 162). However, the Public Health Service, the United States Fish and Wildlife Service, and representatives of local interests have indicated a strong desire for a model study to determine the full effect of the barrier on water quality in Jamaica Bay. Such model tests could be undertaken as part of a coordinated design and construction program.

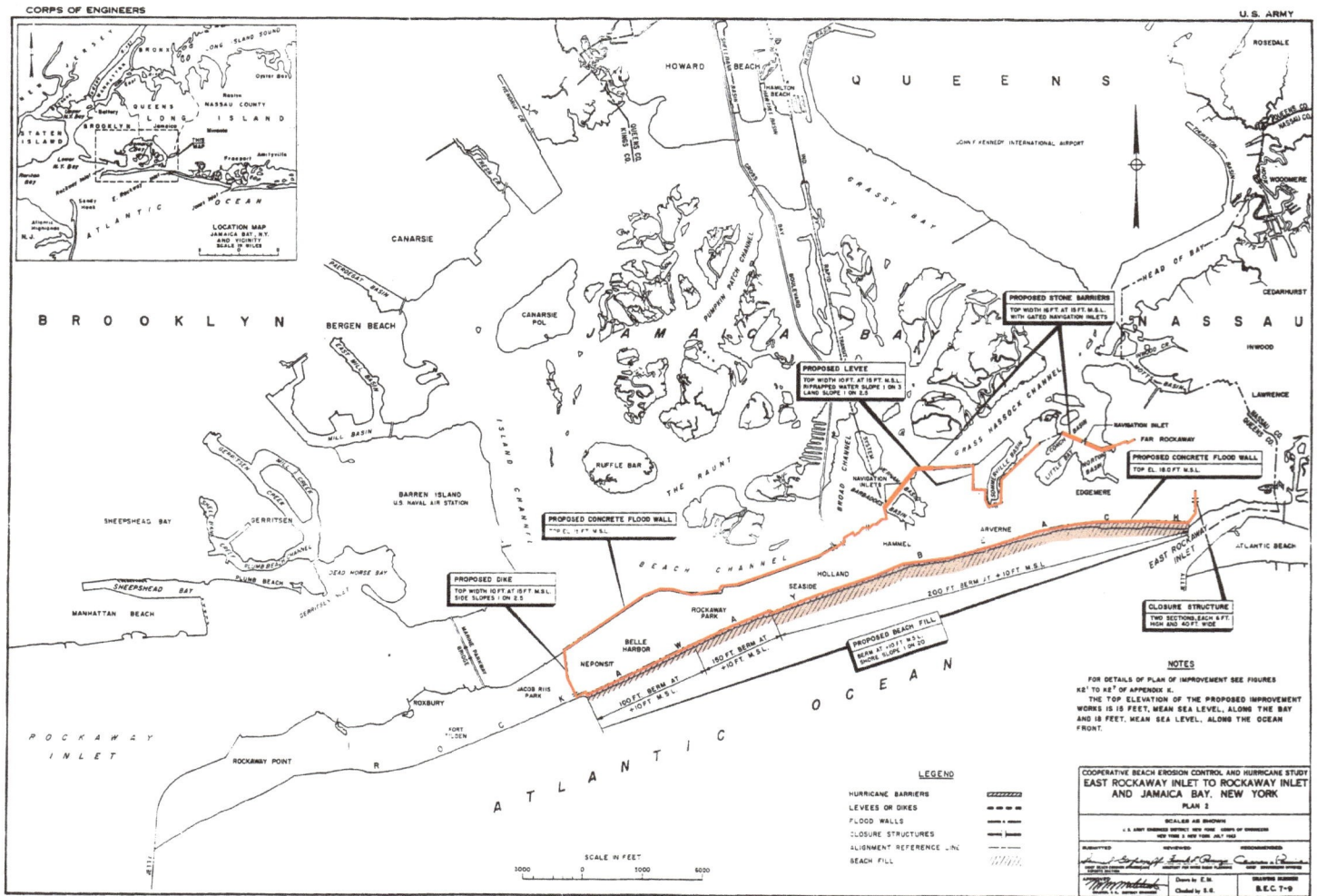

Cooperative Beach Erosion Control and Hurricane Study, 1965
East Rockaway Inlet to Rockaway Inlet and Jamaica Bay, PLAN 2
source: US Army Corps of Engineers, New York District

133. Plan 2. This plan provides for local protection against tidal inundation and wave attack from the ocean and bay between Far Rockaway and the eastern boundary of Jacob Riis Park, as shown on plate 15 of the main report and figures K2^1 to K27 of appendix K.

134. Protection along the ocean front under this plan would consist of the same structures as under Plan 1, as described in paragraph 126.

135. Along Jamaica Bay, the proposed improvement would have a top elevation of 15 feet, mean sea level, for its entire length. Between the east boundary of Jacob Riis Park and the Cross Bay Parkway Bridge about 15,300 feet of concrete wall with a recurved face would be provided. The improvement would be tied into the approaches to the Cross Bay Parkway Bridge.

136. Between the Cross Bay Parkway Bridge and the embankment of the Rockaway Line of the New York City Transit Authority, the improvement would consist of about 2,200 feet of wall and 950 feet of levee. Stoplog structures would be provided at Beach 92nd Street and between Beach 87th and Beach 88th Streets. East of the transit facility embankment, a 3,350-foot long earth fill barrier with rock faces and toes would be constructed across Barbadoes and Vernam Basins, and a stoplog structure would be provided near Sommerville Basin. The barrier structure would have a top elevation of 15 feet above mean sea level, a top width of 16 feet and 1 on 1.5 side slopes. A 50-foot wide navigation opening extending to 15 feet below mean low water would be provided into Barbadoes Basin. During storms this opening would be closed by 50-foot stoplogs. An opening 100 feet wide extending to 16 feet below mean low water would be provided into Vernam Basin. This opening would be closed by a 100-foot wide sector gate.

137. The improvement would be carried to high ground in the park north of the Edgemere Houses on Almeda Avenue, with about 6,500 feet of levee and 2,700 feet of wall. East of this park, a 2,650-foot long barrier would be constructed across Norton Basin. It would have the same cross-section as the Barbadoes-Vernam barrier and the same type of navigation opening as that provided for Barbadoes Basin. The protective works would be tied into high ground with 900 feet of levee improvement and the raising of 300 feet of Bessemund Avenue. The levee would have a top width of 10 feet and side slopes of 1 on 3 and 1 on 2.5 on the exposed side and protected side, respectively. The exposed side would be protected with riprap.

138. Interceptor sewers would be provided in the improvement area lying between Cross Bay Parkway and Jacob Riis Park to collect the flow from the existing sewers that now empty into Jamaica Bay. The collected flow would be carried to four pumping stations located along Beach Channel Drive in the vicinity of Beach 108th, Beach 116th, Beach 128th and Beach 144th Streets. Each of the proposed pumping stations would have a capacity of 12,000 gallons per minute and would pump the collected water over the top of the improvement into Jamaica Bay. The existing outfalls would operate at normal tidal levels, and flap gates and slide gates would prevent back-flow during periods of high tide when pumps would discharge the flow into Jamaica Bay.

139. To the east of Cross Bay Parkway, interceptor sewers would be provided to carry storm water discharges to Barbadoes, Vernam, and Norton Basins, which would serve as ponding areas. Two 12,500 gallons per minute vertical propeller pumps would be installed in one of each of the abutments of the Barbadoes Basin and Vernam Basin navigation openings. Two 25,000 gallons per minute pumps of the same type would be provided at Norton Basin. These pumps would maintain the water surface of the basin below the stage of zero damage.

140. The proposed improvement has been designed to provide complete protection from ocean and bay inundation to the inclosed area against a tide of 11 feet above mean sea level at Fort Hamilton. This is 2.4 feet higher than the maximum of record tide which occurred during hurricane Donna on 12 September 1960. Consideration was given to providing hurricane protection against storms of greater intensity by use of local protection works, but it was found that such a degree of protection would greatly interfere with local activities.

141. This plan would provide the same types of recreational benefits along the ocean front as plan 1 (see paragraph 132). In addition, recreational boats would be afforded a sheltered anchorage in Barbadoes, Vernam and Norton Basins.

12

Cooperative Beach Erosion Control and Hurricane Study, 1965
East Rockaway Inlet to Rockaway Inlet and Jamaica Bay, PLAN 3
source: US Army Corps of Engineers, New York District

142. <u>Plan 3</u>. This plan provides for local protection of the Howard Beach area near the northeast shore of Jamaica Bay by levees, barriers, and interior drainage facilities. It should be noted that this plan would not be needed if plan 1 is adopted. The plan is shown on plate 16 of the main report and figure K3 of appendix K.

143. The proposed improvement would start at high ground north of the Howard Beach Station of the Rockaway Line of the New York City Transit Authority. A levee would run south for 4,300 feet, cross the tracks of the Rockaway line and then run west for a distance of 800 feet. The levee would have a top elevation of 15 feet above mean sea level, a top width of 10 feet, and side slopes of 1 on 3 and 1 on 2.5 on the exposed and protected sides, respectively. The 1 on 3 slope would be covered with riprap. A closure structure would be provided at the point where the levee crosses the transit facility tracks.

144. At Hawtree Basin, a 700-foot long earth fill barrier with rock faces and toes would be constructed. The barrier would have a top elevation of 15 feet, mean sea level, a top width of 16 feet, and 1 on 1.5 side slopes. A 50-foot wide navigation opening extending to 15 feet below mean low water, which would be closed by stoplogs during storms would be provided in the barrier. The levee improvement would continue west along the bay for about 1,000 feet to Shellbank Basin. A 400-foot long barrier with the same dimensions and navigation opening as that at Hawtree Basin would be provided across Shellbank Basin. The improvement would be carried to high ground near the intersection of Linden Boulevard and 79th Street with about 8,950 feet of levee. The levee would have the same cross-section as that described in the preceding paragraph.

145. Ponding for the interior drainage would be provided in Shellbank and Hawtree Basins. Two 25,000 gallons per minute propeller pumps would be installed in one abutment of each of the navigation openings within these basins to maintain the ponds below the stage of zero damage. A pumping station with a capacity of 12,000 gallons per minute would be provided to handle the interior drainage from the west reach of the improvement north of Shore Parkway.

146. This improvement would provide complete protection from tidal inundation to Howard Beach against a tide of 11 feet above mean sea level at Fort Hamilton, as described in paragraph 140.

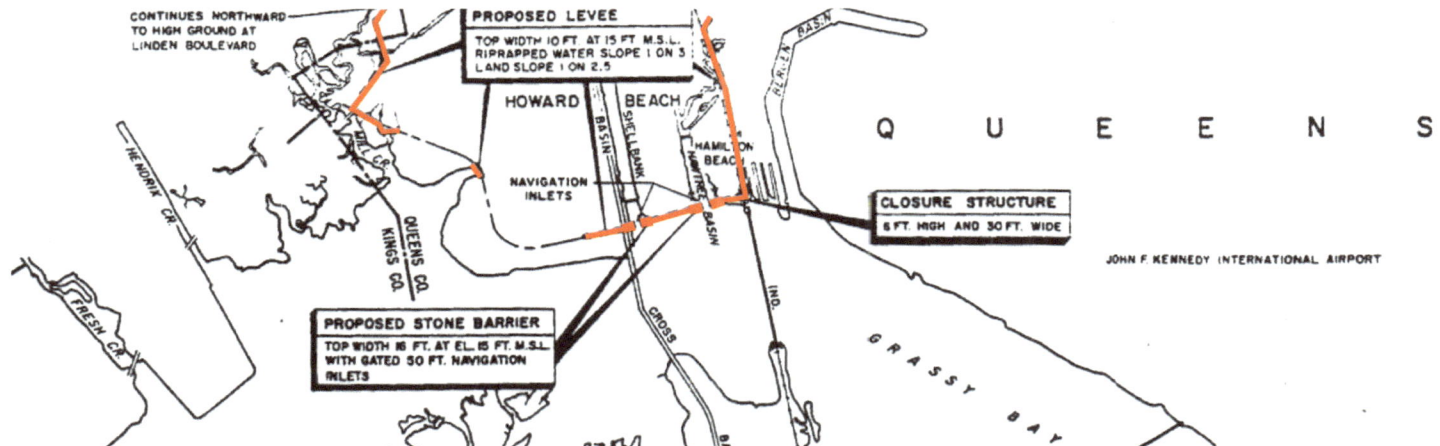

Cooperative Beach Erosion Control and Hurricane Study, 1965
East Rockaway Inlet to Rockaway Inlet and Jamaica Bay, PLAN 3 (detail at Howard Beach)
source: US Army Corps of Engineers, New York District

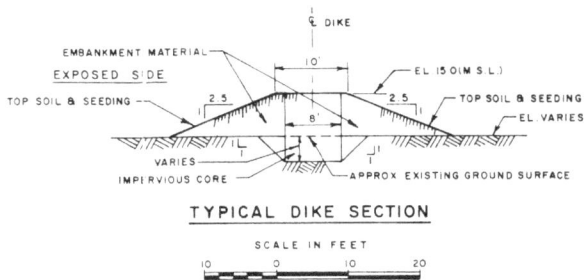

TYPICAL DIKE SECTION

SCALE IN FEET

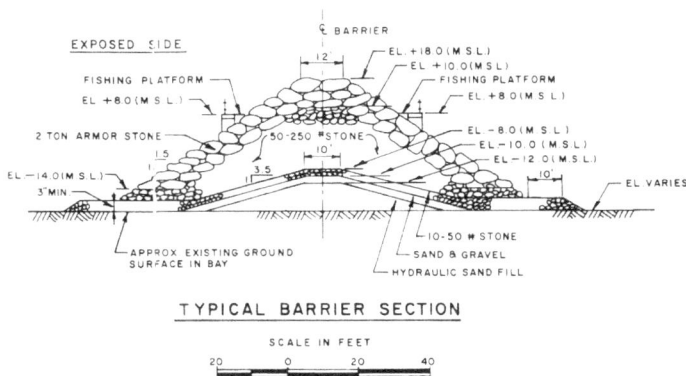

TYPICAL BARRIER SECTION

SCALE IN FEET

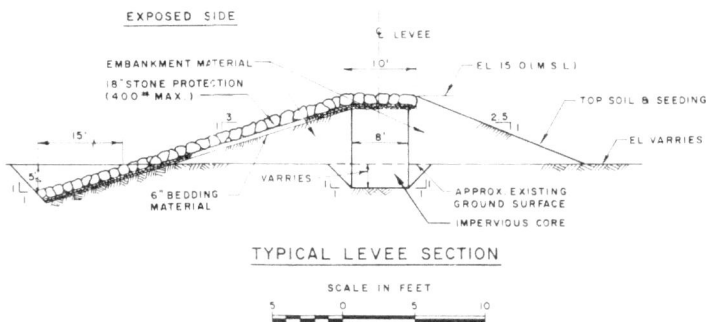

TYPICAL LEVEE SECTION

SCALE IN FEET

Typical sections of proposed hurricane barriers and bayshore dikes and
levees at Jamaica Bay, 1965
source: US Army Corps of Engineers, New York District

117. _Hurricane barriers._ The considered barrier at the entrance
to Jamaica Bay would be a rock and sand fill structure with a top elevation of 18 feet above mean sea level, a top width of 12 feet, and side
slopes of 1 on 1.5. A 600-foot wide navigation opening extending to 40
feet below mean low water (42.5 feet below sea level) would be provided. During spring tide conditions, velocities through this opening
would not exceed 4.5 knots which are considered suitable for navigation
purposes. Two rolling dam type gates would partially close the opening
to a width of 300 feet during storms. With this reduced opening, a standard project hurricane surge of 12.3 feet would be attenuated to 5.2 feet
inside the bay, which is about zero damage stage. At such a time, velocities at the gate structure would reach about 25 feet per second. Rock
paving of the channel bottom would be provided to prevent scouring.

118. Under the local protection plans, barriers across Barbadoes,
Vernam and Norton Basins would be earth fill structures with rock faces
and toes. They would have top elevations of 15 feet above mean sea level,
top widths of 16 feet, and 1 on 1.5 side slopes. Navigation openings,
50 feet wide and extending to 15 feet below mean low water, would be provided into Norton Basin and Barbadoes Basin. These openings would be
closed by 50-foot wide stoplogs. Vernam Basin would have an opening 100
feet wide extending to 16 feet below mean low water. This opening would
be closed by a 100-foot wide sector gate.

119. At Shellbank Basin and Hawtree Basin, located at Howard Beach,
barriers would be earth fill structures with rock faces and toes. The
top elevations of the structures would be 15 feet above mean sea level,
the top width would be 16 feet, and side slope would be 1 on 1.5. Navigation openings 50 feet wide would extend to 15 feet below mean low water.
These openings would be closed by 50-foot wide stoplogs.

120. _Bayshore local protection._ The design of concrete floodwalls,
levees and dikes, has followed published standards of the Office of the
Chief of Engineers. The top elevation of the structures has been set at
15 feet above mean sea level to allow for wave run-up. Floodwalls would
be provided with recurved faces to reduce wave run-up. Levees would have
a slope of 1 on 3 on the bay side, protected with riprap, and a slope of
1 on 2.5 on the landward side. Dikes would have slopes of 1 on 2.5 on
both sides.

121. _Interior drainage._ Interior drainage systems consisting of
pumps, reinforced concrete pipes, and tide gates would be required to
handle surface runoff which would be intercepted by the considered local
protection work. The systems have been designed to accommodate a 10-
year storm, as given in the U. S. Weather Bureau Technical Paper No. 25,
titled "Rainfall Intensity-Duration-Frequency Curves", occurring at the
time of spring tide.

116. *Ocean front protection.* Ocean front protection would consist of a beach backed by a wall consisting of steel sheet piling encased in concrete. The beach would have a minimum berm width of 100 feet at an elevation of 10 feet above mean sea level based on model tests by the Beach Erosion Board and foreshore slopes of 1 on 20 and 1 on 30, which are typical of the existing slopes in the study area. The beach would be widened to provide a berm up to 200 feet in some areas to provide for recreational needs. Widening to the prescribed dimensions would be provided only where the desired widths do not already exist. Computations indicate that wave run-up on the wall would be about 5 feet above still water level, or to an elevation of 16 feet above mean sea level. However, to allow for the possibility that the beach berm may be eroded by a severe storm occurring prior to the design storm, and because of the possible severe effects of the failure of this structure, its top elevation has been raised by 2 feet to 18 feet above mean sea level. Under the plan which provides for the hurricane barrier at the entrance to Jamaica Bay, such a wall, which forms an integral part of the plan, would provide the same degree of protection against the standard project hurricane as the barrier itself (see paragraph 113).

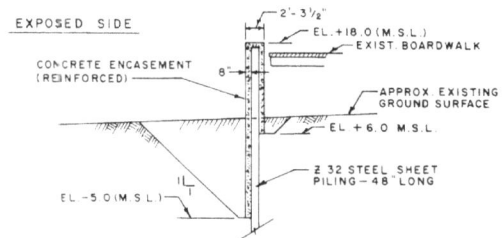

FLOODWALL—ALONG OCEAN FRONT

SCALE IN FEET

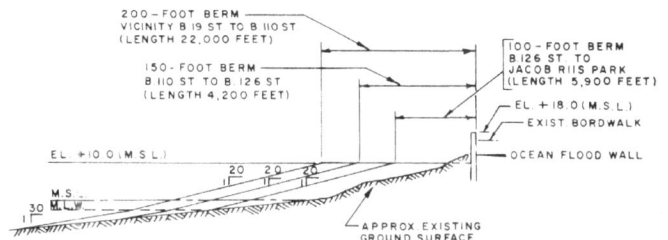

TYPICAL PROFILES OF BEACH FILL

SCALE IN FEET

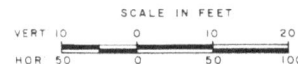

Typical sections of proposed floodwall and beach fill at the Rockaway Peninsula ocean front, 1965
source: US Army Corps of Engineers, New York District

NATURAL AND NATURE-BASED FEATURES (NNBF)

These features are considered as part of the US Army Corps of Engineers' current array of strategies for coastal storm risk management.

source: Adapted from USACE Directorate of Civil Works, "Coastal Risk Reduction and Resilience: Using the Full Array of Measures," 2014

Oyster and Coral Reefs

source: http://aquaviews.net

Benefits / Processes
- Break offshore waves
- Attenuate wave energy
- Slow inland water transfer

Performance Factors
- Reef width, elevation and roughness

Maritime Forests/Shrub Communities

Benefits / Processes
- Wave attenuation and/or dissipation
- Shoreline erosion stabilization
- Soil retention

Performance Factors
- Vegetation height and density
- Forest dimension
- Sediment composition
- Platform elevation

Benefits / Processes
- Break offshore waves
- Attenuate wave energy
- Slow inland water transfer
- Increase infiltration

Performance Factors
- Marsh, wetland, or SAV elevation and continuity
- Vegetation type and density

Vegetated Features:
Salt Marshes, Wetlands, Submerged Aquatic Vegetation (SAV)

Benefits / Processes
- Wave attenuation and/or dissipation
- Sediment stabilization

Performance Factors
- Island elevation, length, and width
- Land cover
- Breach susceptibility
- Proximity to mainland shore

Barrier Islands

Benefits / Processes
- Break offshore waves
- Attenuate wave energy
- Slow inland water transfer

Performance Factors
- Berm height and width
- Beach slope
- Sediment grain size and supply
- Dune height, crest, width
- Presence of vegetation

Dunes and Beaches

United States Patent Office.

DEVICE FOR SECURING AND
FEEDING SOFT CRABS
Constantin Drexler
US Patent No. 72177
December 17, 1867

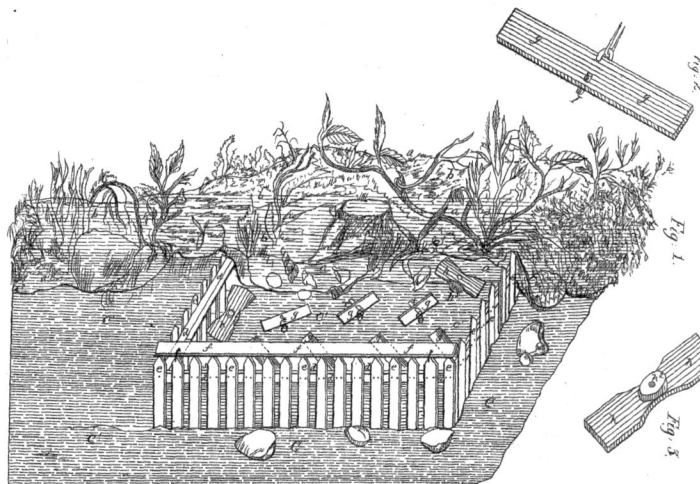

Figure 1 represents, in perspective, the apparatus or contrivance employed for the purpose.

Inventor:
Constantin Drexler

Witnesses:
M. A. Gallaher
Edward Meddr

Description of my Crustaceorium and Piscatorium.

The letters of reference *a a b b*, fig. 1, mark a representation of a river-shore or margin, having a gradual-sloping hard bottom, *c' c' c' c'*. Letters *d d d d* mark suitable substantial rails, forming a framing of two ends and one front, having affixed thereto, at intervals of about one inch, upright boards, palings, or stakes *e e e e*, extending down the full depth of water, close to or driven into the bottom thereof; the upper ends being pointed, if desired, and rising out of and above the surface of the water not less than two feet clear of high tide. These palings or narrow boards must be securely nailed to the framing; the whole forming an enclosure two hundred feet long by one hundred wide, varying, however, in length and width, with more or less area, as convenience, location, and circumstances may suit—an enclosure four hundred feet long by two hundred feet wide, affording eighty thousand square feet in area, with sufficient volume of water to accommodate conveniently forty thousand living crabs without crowding.

PROPAGATION OF OYSTERS
Andrew B. Hendryx
US Patent No. 611199
September 20, 1898

The present method most generally employed in propagating oysters is to catch the spat on oyster-shells or broken stone dumped
20 upon the surface of the oyster-bed.

As is well known, the oyster-spat first floats near the surface of the water and gradually settles and is caught by the shells or stones. It is equally well known that but a small pro-
25 portion of the spat is caught at all and that a large proportion of that which is caught and allowed to set is lost by the washing of sand and mud over the bed by storms and currents and by devastation of starfish.
30 The object of this invention is to provide surfaces above the bottom of the bed to which the spat will readily attach itself, and whereby the oysters will be supported above the bottom of the bed and therefore out of reach
35 of starfish, which it is believed do not attack oysters unless resting upon the bottom of the bed; and the invention consists in temporarily anchoring or otherwise securing masses of brush, which when first set out will float
40 upright in the water, and hence be in a position to catch the spat as it is drifted about through the water by the currents.

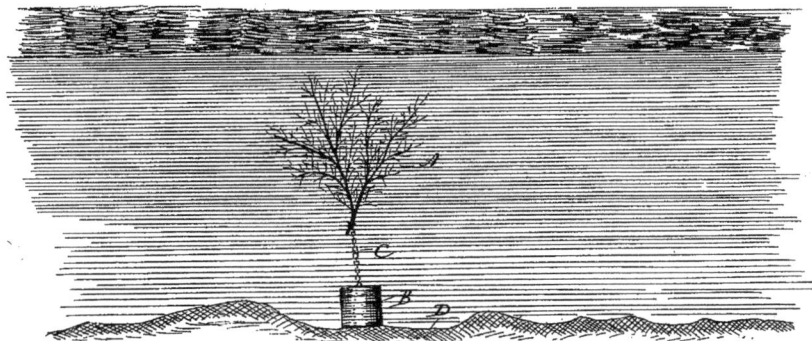

drawing constitutes part of this specification and represents a side view of a single brush anchored in accordance with my invention.

United States Patent Office.

APPARATUS FOR THE
CULTIVATION OF OYSTERS
Luis Falero
US Patent No. 413503
October 22, 1889

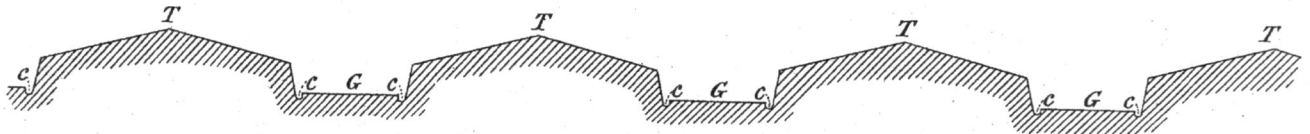

Fig: 1.

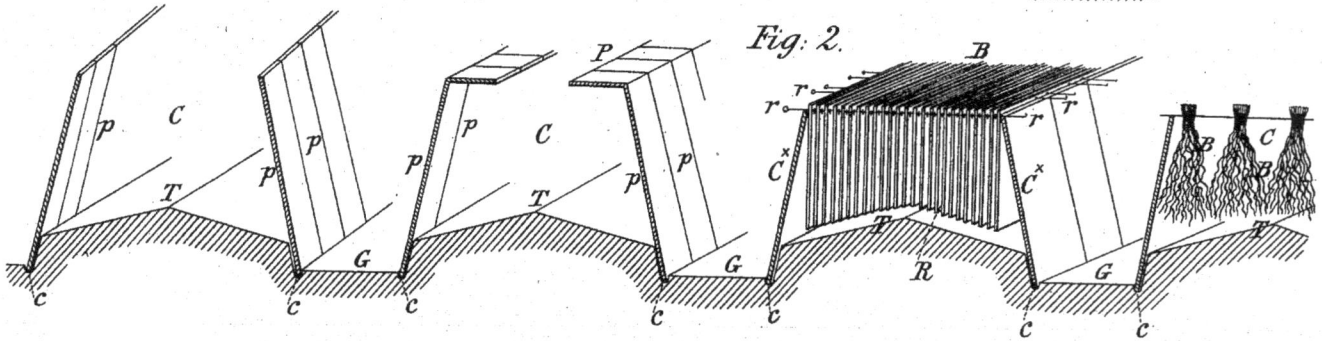

Fig: 2.

Witnesses.

Inventor.
Luis Faléro.
By James L. Norris.
Atty.

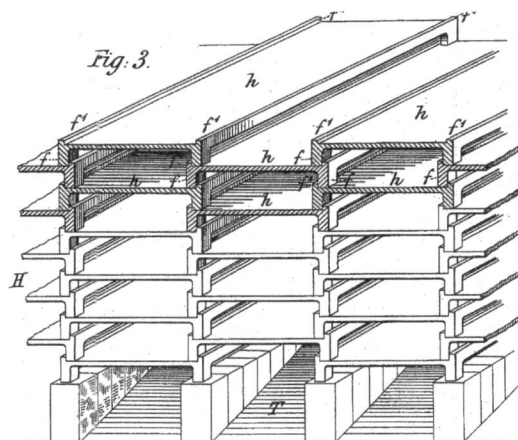
Fig. 3.

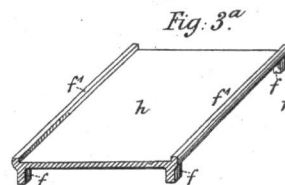
Fig. 3.ᵃ

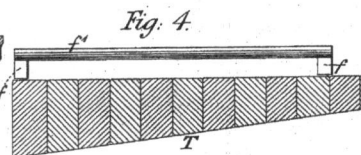
Fig. 4.

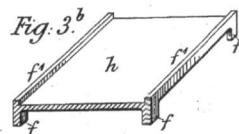
Fig. 3.ᵇ

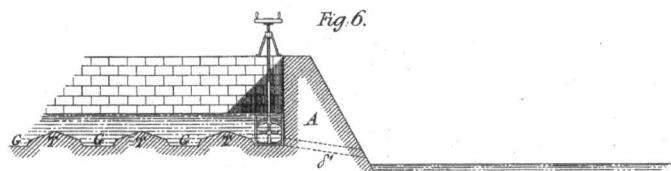
Fig. 6.

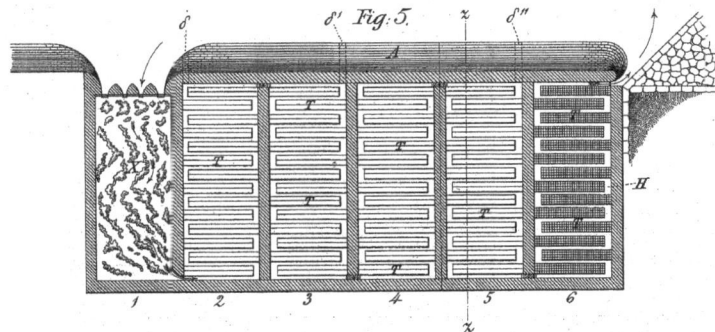
Fig. 5.

My improvements in oyster culture relate to the general installation, as well as to the
10 arrangement of details, of artificial oyster-beds, and are characterized by certain new features, hereinafter described, whereby the breeding, rearing, and fattening of oysters are effected under hygienic conditions, and a
15 greater yield or output for a given bed-surface is obtained. Given a natural or artificial pond or reservoir periodically covered with sea-water at the time of the tides and left dry or partially emptied, when required, by
20 means of water gates and locks, the first condition for a good rearing consists in the construction of a bottom upon which mud cannot accumulate, (at least in places where the oysters are deposited,) and which permits by
25 its disposition of the easy and thorough cleansing of its whole extent without disturbing the oysters—disturbance being very prejudicial to them. Mud being the most mortal enemy to the oyster, the spat can successfully de-
30 velop even among the mother oysters, provided the bottom be always free from mud, especially in closed spaces or ponds where the mollusks while still young are protected from their marine enemies.
35 Artificial oyster-beds are, as a rule, at present made with a flat or curved bottom with slight inclines in whatever manner the bottom may be prepared upon which the oysters are deposited in more or less uniform layers. All
40 these bottoms ultimately tend to silt up, even in the most perfectly-constructed installations, and the accumulated deposits will at last smother the oysters if care be not taken to clean the bottom frequently. This operation,
45 which is always difficult and costly, generally necessitates the disturbing of the oysters and always renders difficult or prevents the collection of the spat.
And in order that my invention may be
50 clearly understood, I will proceed to describe the same with reference to the accompanying drawings, in which—

United States Patent Office.

IMPROVEMENT IN OBTAINING
FOUNDATIONS FOR MARINE OR
OTHER STRUCTURES
Edward Manico
US Patent No. 73617
January 21, 1868

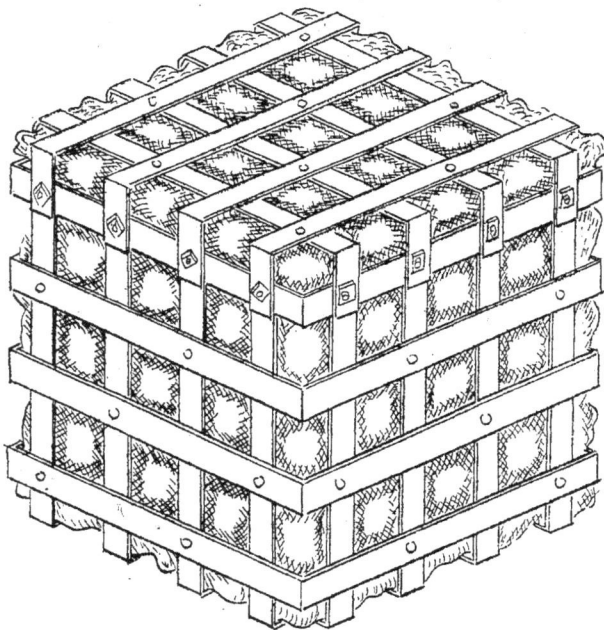

WITNESSES.

Jno Beardwood, Staff Commander R.N.

Thomas R Hehl   Master R N

INVENTOR

Edward Manico

———— • ————

I call my invention a "*caisson de fer*." It will be perceived that it is adapted in an especial manner to fixing and securing foundations for permanent sea-works on dangerous and exposed coasts, where masonry will not stand the effects of the sea, and where there is no escape for vessels that are driven upon such coasts, because it presents the means of creating artificial harbors where nature has not provided them, and also that it is applicable to banks of canals, to the re-creation of land washed away by the sea, and for sea-works on sandy coasts, where foundations for breakwaters cannot be obtained by any other means.

APPARATUS FOR PROTECTING THE BANKS OF STREAMS

William H. Bell
US Patent No. 239920
April 12, 1881

This invention relates to means for fending off currents, breaking eddies, preventing erosion of banks, and causing alluvial-bearing
15 streams to deposit sediment over, between, and in the fenders, by which process the banks will be protected and accretions formed.

My invention consists in a fender for submersion, constructed of brush, bagasse, or other
20 suitable material, arranged in layers having the shape of a cross.

My invention further consists in a fender-block composed of wooden frames, in which brush or bagasse or other suitable material is
25 arranged in layers crosswise, in combination with weighted material between the same.

My invention further consists in means, hereinafter described, for lowering the fender-blocks.

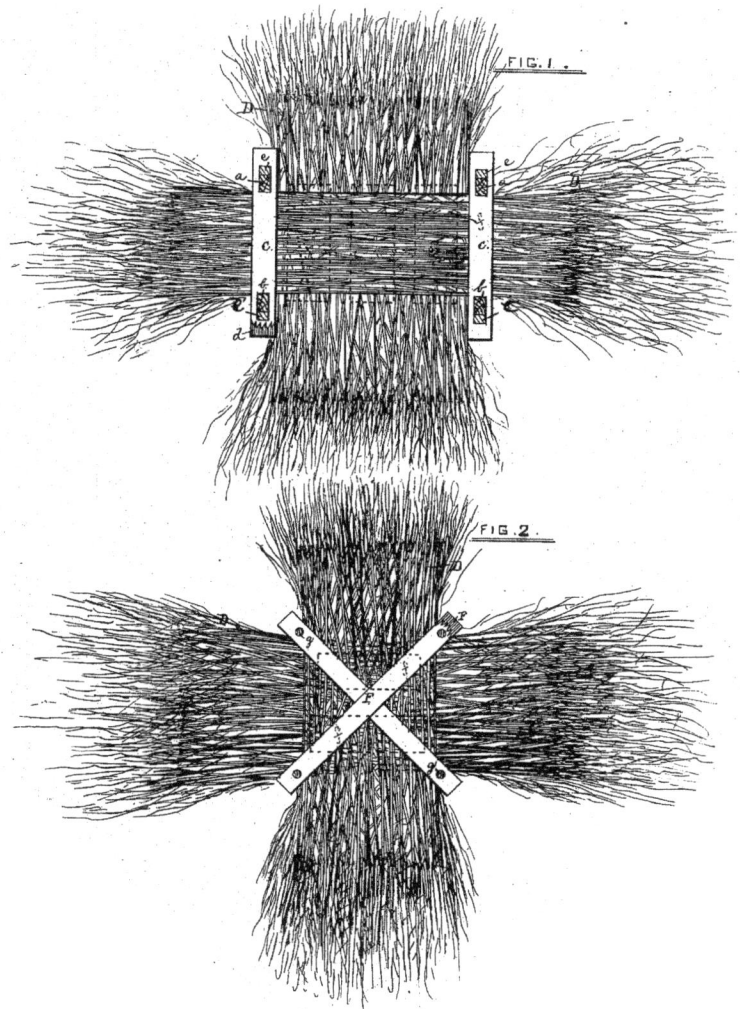

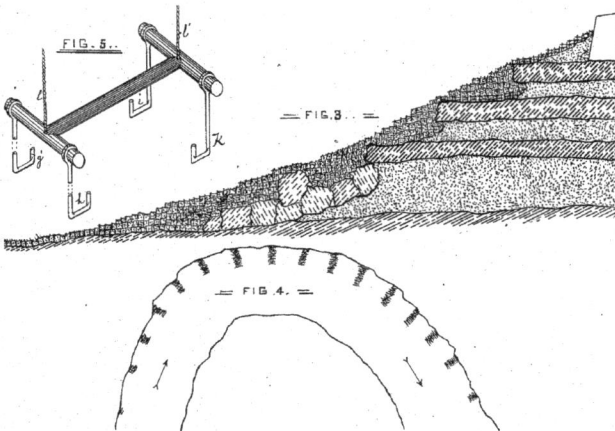

FIG. 1.

FIG. 2.

FIG. 5.

FIG. 3.

FIG. 4.

WITNESSES.
J. C. Hubbell
J. C. Clarke

INVENTOR.
W. H. Bell
BY H. N. Jenkins
ATTORNEY

DEVICE FOR PREVENTING
BANKS FROM CAVING
Daniel H. Solomon
US Patent No. 449185
March 31, 1891

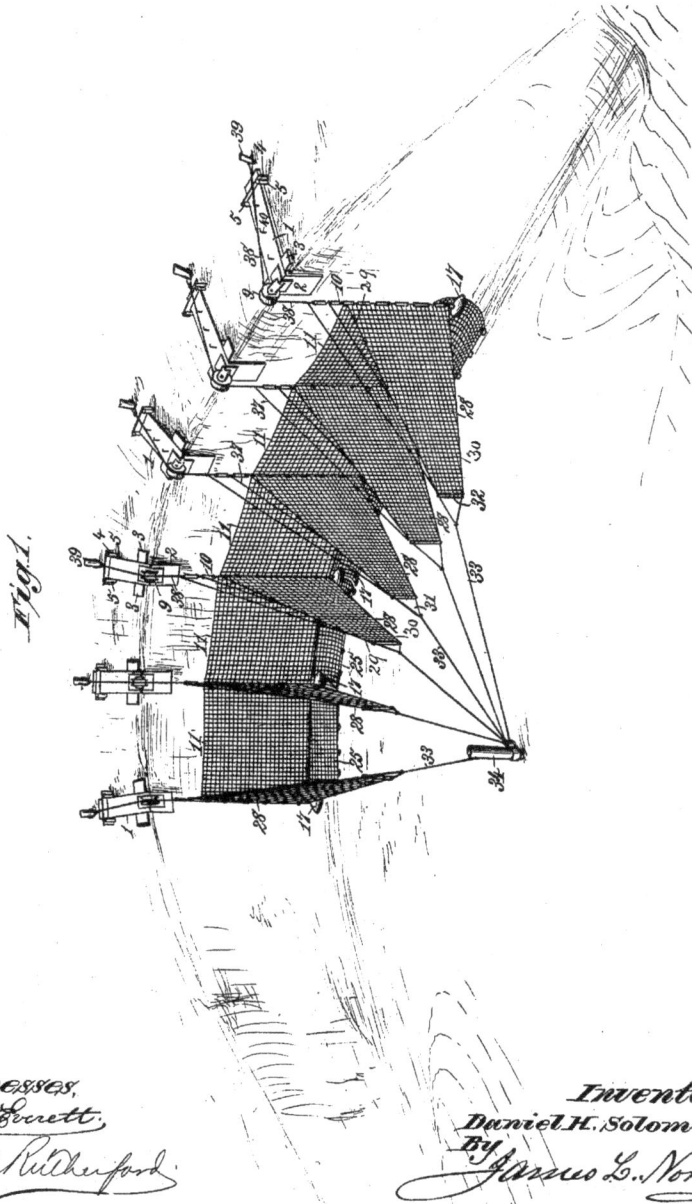

Fig.1.

Witnesses,
Phil Everett.
J. A. Rutherford.

Inventor:
Daniel H. Solomon.
By
James L. Norris.
Atty.

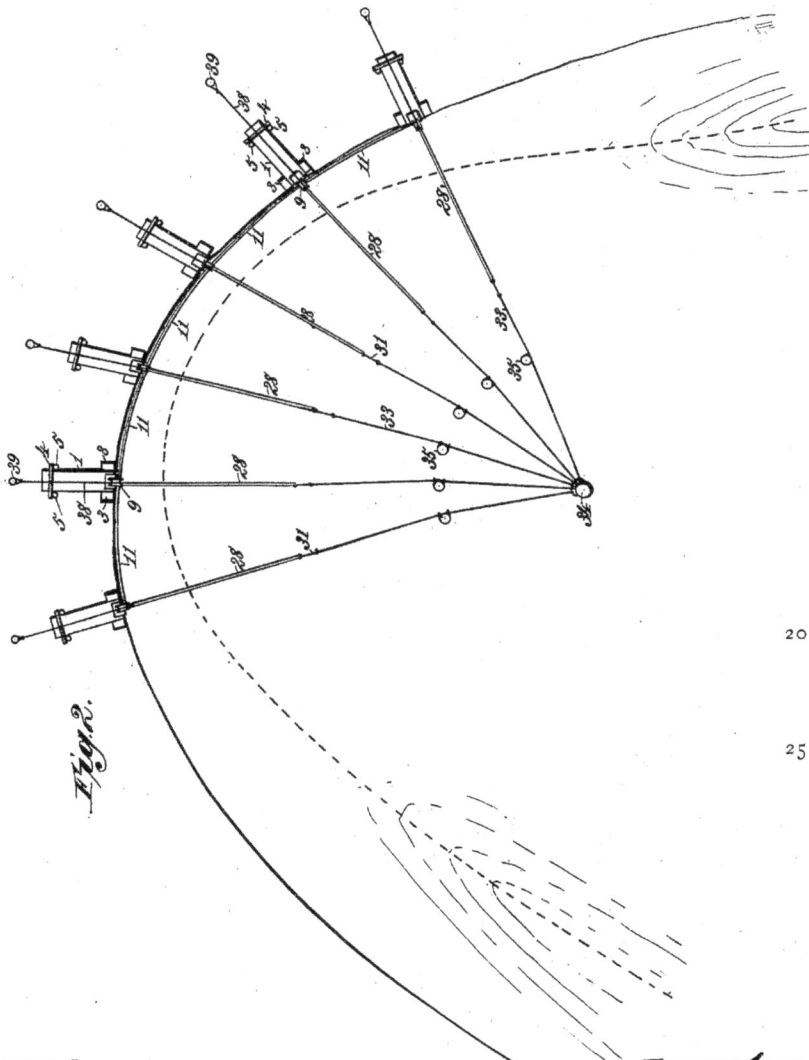

Fig. 2.

The invention is particularly designed to protect and restore the bank on the concave
20 side of a bend in a sediment-bearing river flowing in an alluvial and yielding bed of its own formation, but is applicable to the improvement of navigation and other useful purposes in various situations by warding off
25 or resisting the destructive action of strong currents directed against the bank and by encouraging the deposit of restorative material in comparatively still water at the foot of the bank.

Witnesses.
Robert Everett.
J. A. Rutherford

Inventor.
Daniel H. Solomon.
By
James L. Norris.
Atty.

UNITED STATES PATENT OFFICE.

MEANS FOR PRODUCING
SAND BEACHES
William L. Averill
US Patent No. 618319
January 24, 1899

Fig. 1.

Fig. 2.

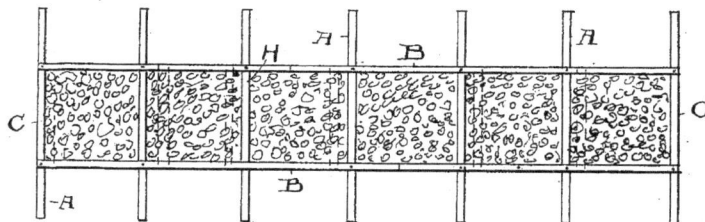

Fig. 3.

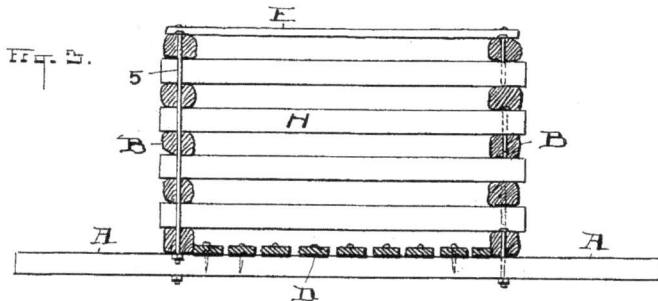

What I claim is—

1. A series of sand-building cribs to form beaches, consisting of cribs spaced apart to leave waterways between their ends, said cribs each formed with a series of subdivisions having open-work walls and bottoms, and stone filling said subdivisions to hold the cribs down in the water, and each crib having projections on its base along both sides to prevent tilting, substantially as described.

2. A sand-building crib for water-washed shores, consisting of a series of bottom timbers projecting at each side beyond the side walls of the crib such distance as to prevent the crib from tilting and upsetting when it settles to position, a series of walled compartments constituting said crib having fixed bottoms and zigzag dividing-walls, and bolts fastening the walls together at their corners, substantially as described.

3. The means herein described to promote beach-building along bodies of water by the action of the water, consisting of a series of weighted cribs placed in the water substantially parallel with the shore-line and at such distance from the shore as will promote sand-drifting on the shore side of said cribs, the said cribs being separated at their ends sufficiently to afford a free flow for tide-water or the like back and forth in said spaces, substantially as described.

ATTEST
R. Buver
H. E. Mudra.

INVENTOR
William L. Averill
BY H. J. Fisher
ATTY

MEANS FOR MAKING BEACH
James Sutherland
US Patent No. 421631
February 18, 1890

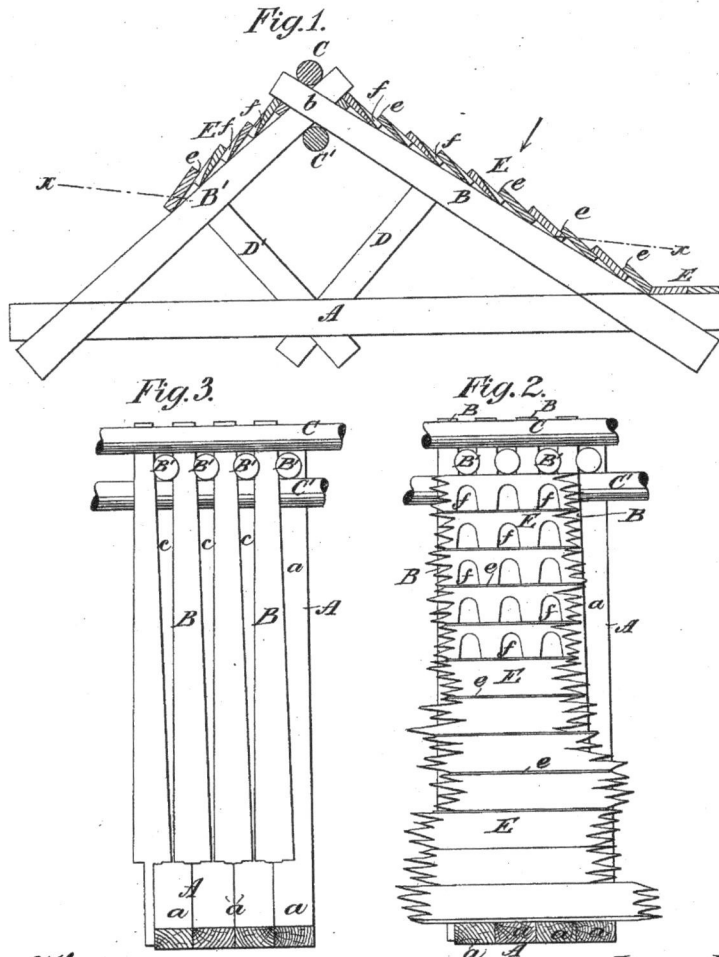

Fig. 1.

Fig. 3.

Fig. 2.

Witnesses:-
D. H. Haywood
C. L. Sundgren

Inventor:-
James Sutherland
by his attorneys
Brown Griswold

My improvement relates to means for causing the accumulation and retention of sand
10 which may be washed up upon the sea-beach by the action of the waves, the operation being usually termed "making beach."

I will describe in detail my improvement, and then point out the novel features in
15 claims.

In the accompanying drawings, Figure 1 is a sectional elevation of a structure embodying my improvement. Fig. 2 is a face view of the same broken away to save space and
20 looking in the direction of the arrow, Fig. 1. Fig. 3 is a view similar to Fig. 2, certain planking with which the structure is faced being removed.

It will be observed that the structure has a hollow interior and that it presents a closed lower portion to the sea. It may be made in
20 sections of any desired length.

In operation the lower portion of the structure is embedded for a distance in the sand, say to about the depth of the dotted line x, Fig. 1. The incoming waves carry with them
25 a quantity of sand which they wash up along the inclined plane forming the face of the structure. Sand accumulates upon the ridges e and falls down through the openings made by the grooves or recesses f into the interior
30 of the structure. Such sand as may pass over to the rear side of the structure will be accumulated upon the ridges formed by the planking upon that side and will pass downwardly through the openings to the interior. Thus
35 the space within the structure will be gradually filled with sand and the whole will become firmly and permanently embedded and will effectively resist the encroachment of the sea and consequent washing away of the
40 beach.

By placing a series of structures of the character described one in advance of the other beach may be rapidly made, as the accumulated sand cannot be again carried out to sea
45 by the returning waves.

UNITED STATES PATENT OFFICE.

SHORE PROTECTOR AND
BEACH BUILDER
Henry F. Knapp
US Patent No. 247065
September 13, 1881

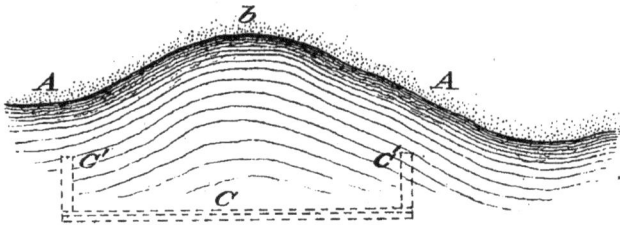

Fig. 1.

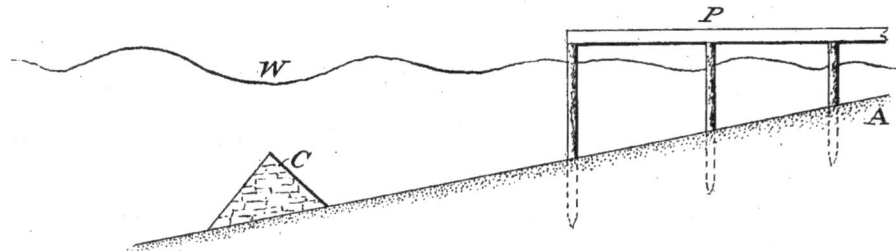

Fig. 3.

Fig. 2.

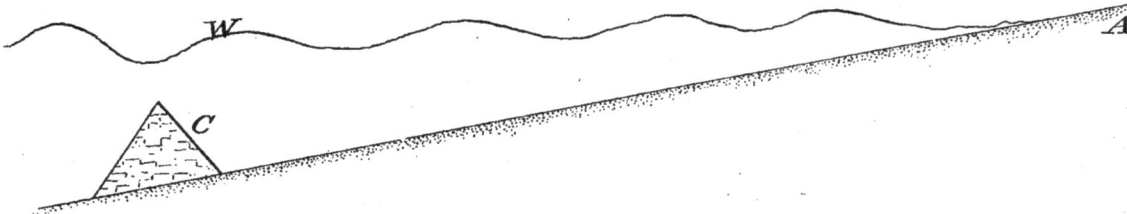

Witnesses:

Inventor.
Henry F. Knapp

UNITED STATES PATENT OFFICE.

FLOATING BREAKWATER FOR HARBORS
OF REFUGE AND TO PROTECT SHORES
FROM SEA WAVE DESTRUCTION

J. Burrows Hyde
US Patent No. 307393
October 28, 1884

My improvement consists in interposing
20 buoyant media that, while floating freely on the
surface of the water, are so anchored that they
will yield to and travel with an advancing
wave, the force of which will be gradually re-
sisted until the float, by passing under the
25 wave, will trip and cause it to fall with its
power neutralized before it can reach the object to be protected.   (See drawings.)

WITNESSES:

Edward E. Ellis
A. Lee Duffy

INVENTOR:

J. Burrows Hyde

BY
O. E. Duffy
ATTORNEY.

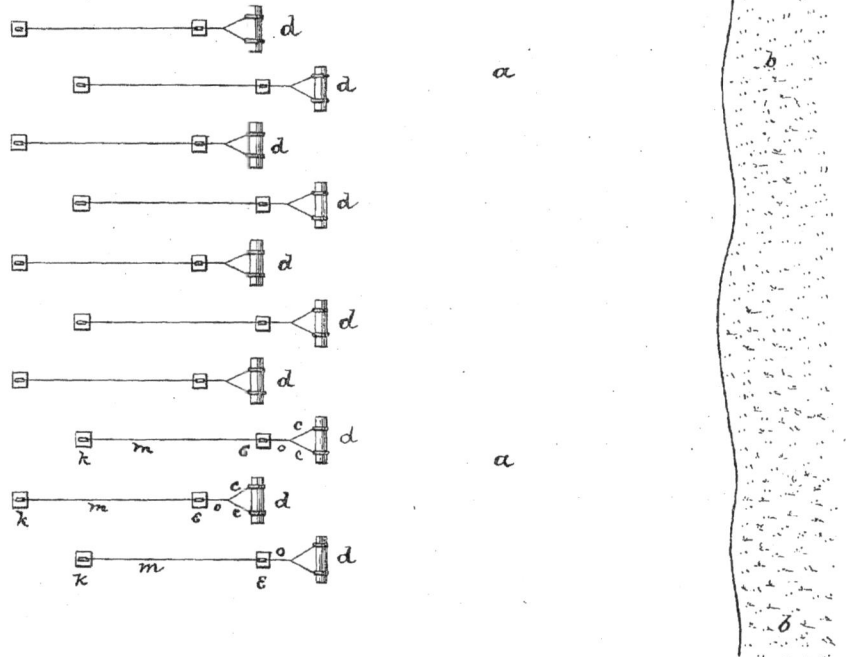

Fig. 1.

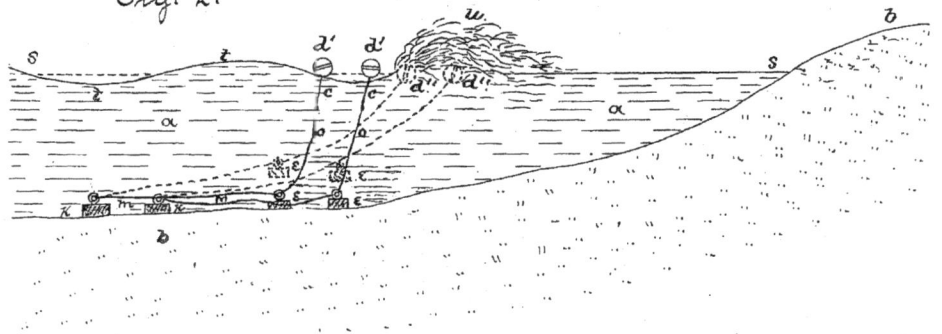

Fig. 2.

UNITED STATES PATENT OFFICE.

FLOOD FENCE
Mathew M. Withrow
US Patent No. 284528
September 4, 1883

I claim as new, and desire to secure by Letters Patent, is—

The combination, in a flood-fence, of the panels A A, having hooks c c near their lower edges, the braces E E, attached to said panels at or near the top on the side opposite to said hooks, the stakes d d, attached to the lower ends of said braces, and the anchors D D, having eyes a, for connection with the hooks c, and provided with the split and bent plates b, all as and for the purpose described.

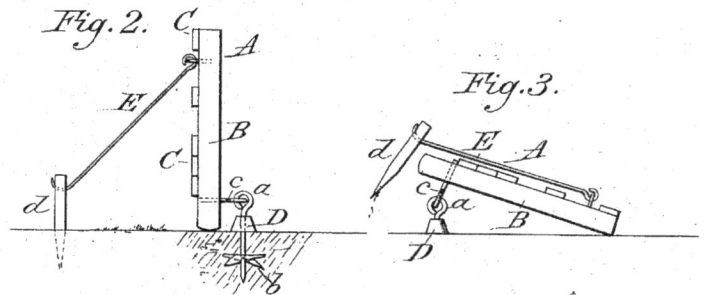

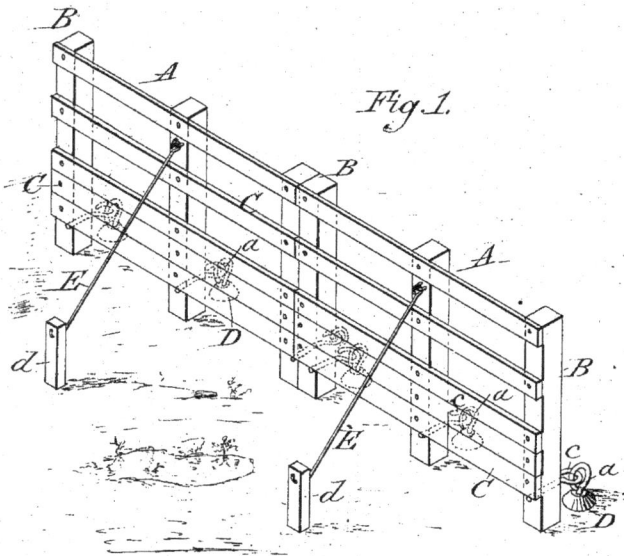

Fig. 2.

Fig. 3.

Fig. 1.

Fig. 4.

Attest:
H. C. Schott
A. R. Brown.

Inventor:
Mathew M. Withrow
C. H. Watson & Co.

BREAKWATER
W. S. Bates
US Patent No. 346140
July 27, 1886

Fig. 1.

Fig. 2.

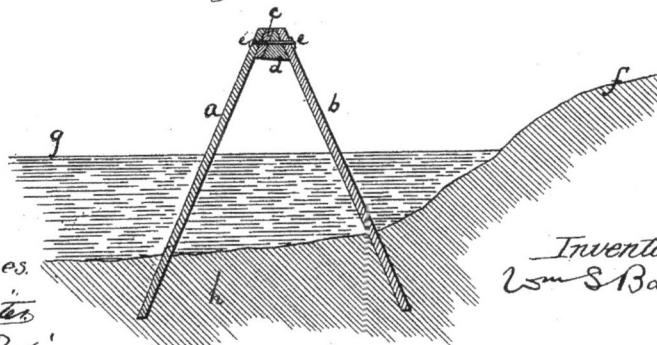

Witnesses.
W. Rossiter
W. C. Minard

Inventor.
Wm S Bates

UNITED STATES PATENT OFFICE.

SEA WALL
David H. Budlong
US Patent No. 254454
March 7, 1882

The letter A indicates the walls of my improved trough, box, or structure. These are composed of hydraulic cement or other cement, and are made in sections of suitable length, set
30 together upon a suitable bottom, B'. The cement which I employ in the formation of the box consists preferably of a compound for which I made application for Letters Patent of the United States on or about the 10th day of
35 January, 1882, although I do not wish to limit myself to the use of such cement. The spaces D between the outer walls of the box or trough as thus constructed are to be filled with the same cement in a plastic or semi-plastic state,
40 as more fully hereinafter specified. The upper part of the space C is intended to be subsequently filled in with cement, as indicated by the letter D', and a cap, E, of cement, to be finally formed upon the top, for the purpose
45 hereinafter specified.

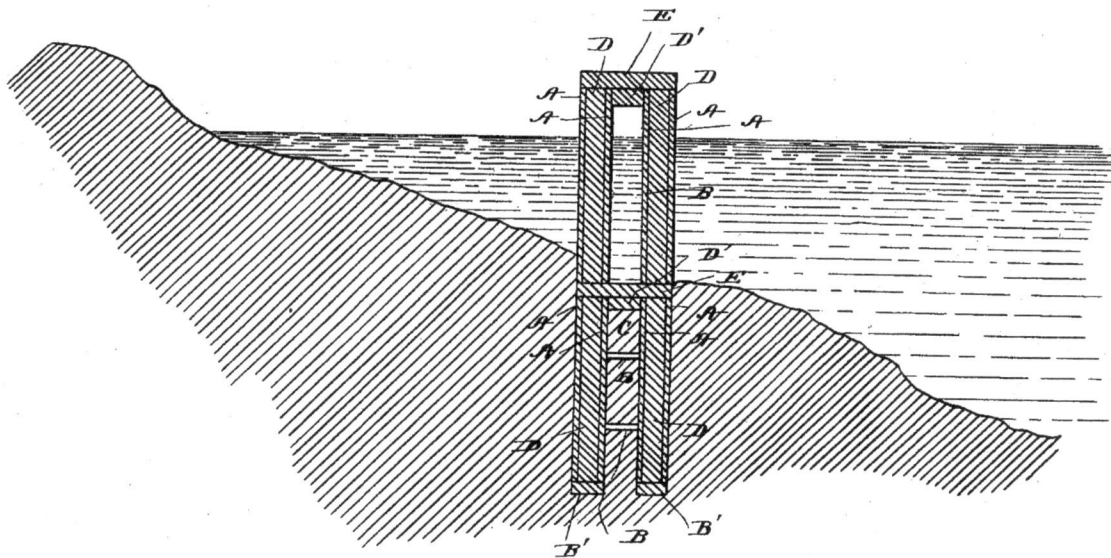

Witnesses.
Edwin L. Yewell.
J. J. McCarthy.

Inventor.
David H. Budlong
by C. M. Alexander,
his Attorney.

United States Patent Office.

MANUFACTURE OF GLASS BUILDING
BLOCKS FOR SEA WALLS
C. W. McLean
US Patent No. 250635
December 6, 1881

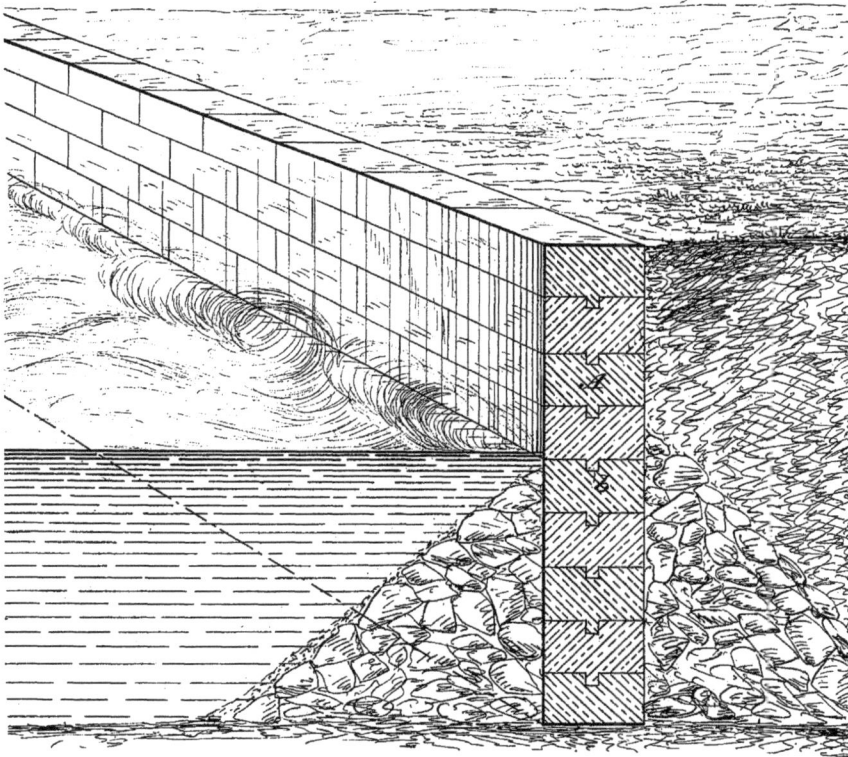

Fig. 1.

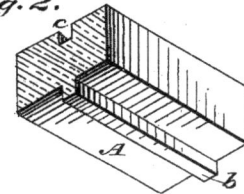

Fig. 2.

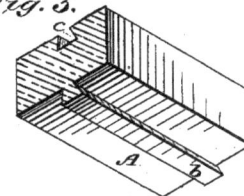

Fig. 3.

WITNESSES
G. Johnson
A. H. Betz.

INVENTOR
Christopher W. McLean,
By J. C. Brecht
his Attorney

UNITED STATES PATENT OFFICE.

JETTY, BREAKWATER, OR
SIMILAR STRUCTURE
Eben Moody Boynton
US Patent No. 315384
April 7, 1885

Fig. 1.

Fig. 2.

Fig. 3.

Fig. 4.

Witnesses:
Jas. F. DuHamel
Walter S. Rodger

Inventor:
Eben Moody Boynton,
by Dodge Son,
his Attys.

METHOD OF BRACING AND LASHING RIPRAP AND JETTY WORK

William H. Harrelson
US Patent No. 554777
February 18, 1896

My invention relates to riprap and jetty
10 work, and my object is to provide a strong,
durable and reliable structure at a minimum
of expense and trouble, which can be successfully projected in a comparatively short time
into the swiftest and deepest of streams, can
15 be used to great advantage to prevent inun-
dations or for all of the various purposes
specified in the Patent No. 426,807, issued to
me April 29, 1890, on riprap and jetty work,
on which this is designed particularly as an
20 improvement.

Witnesses:
G. Y. Thorpe
M. R. Ramley

Inventor:
Wm. H. Harrelson
By Higdon & Higdon
attys.

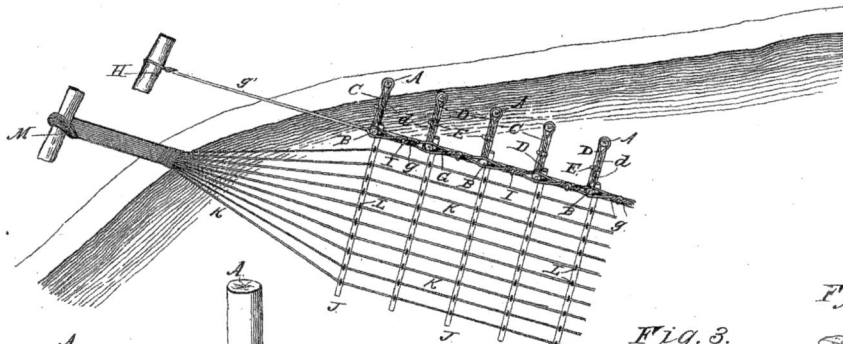
Fig.1.

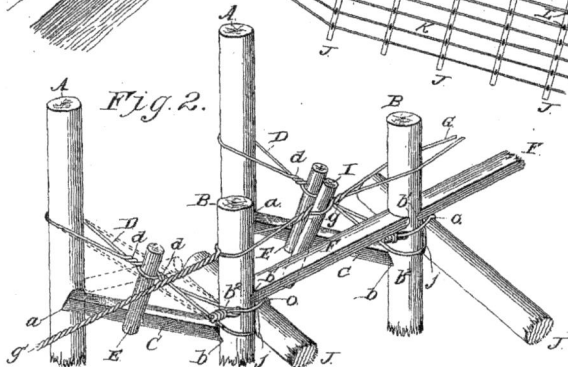
Fig.2.

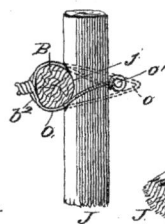
Fig.3.

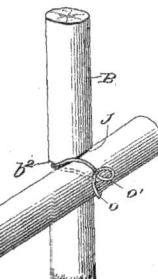
Fig.4.

UNITED STATES PATENT OFFICE.

METHOD OF CONSTRUCTING JETTIES
John C. Goodridge, Jr.
US Patent No. 331127
November 24, 1885

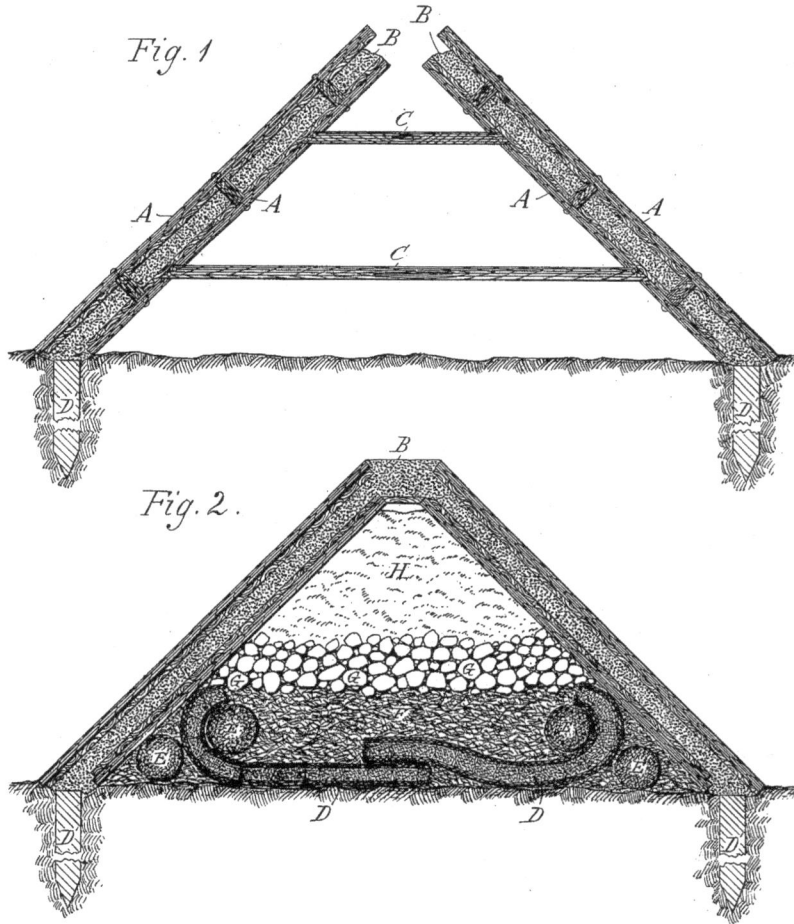

Fig. 1.

Fig. 2.

My invention consists of an improved method of constructing jetties or breakwaters to be used in hydraulic engineering. Hitherto jetties or breakwaters have been made by throwing stones into the water at the desired locality, or of piling, cribs filled with stone, or masses of concrete or stone retained in place by mattresses, fascines, gabions, or similar devices. The use of large masses of stone or concrete thrown into the water at random for this purpose is open to serious objection. To the expense of the material must be added the cost of transportation often from long distances, together with the cost of handling large masses of inconvenient shape and size, while much of the material during the process of laying it finds ultimate lodgment away from instead of upon the work, and thus becomes either wholly or partially lost to use. When wood is used, either wholly or in combination, it is in many localities speedily destroyed by the teredo. The jetty then disintegrates, and its repair becomes difficult. Again, when exposed to the attack of water in motion, the tendency is to undermine these jetties and destroy them by washing away the foundation upon which they rest, and this is the usual process of their destruction.

My invention is intended to provide a cheap and easy method of constructing such jetties or breakwaters, which at the same time provides wholly or in great part against their destruction from any of the causes above set forth, and which facilitates repair, should it be at any time required.

WITNESSES

W. A. Lowe

Harry R. Will

INVENTOR

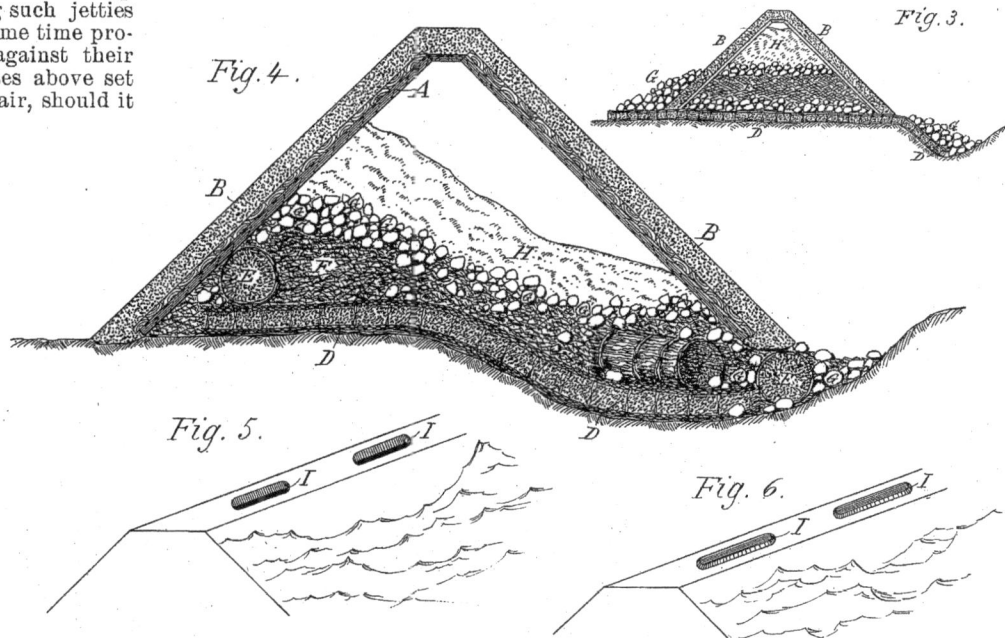

Fig. 4.

Fig. 3.

Fig. 5.

Fig. 6.

www.ingramcontent.com/pod-product-compliance
Lightning Source LLC
Chambersburg PA
CBHW060827270326
41931CB00002B/86

* 9 7 8 1 9 4 2 9 0 0 1 4 6 *